LOVING AND HONORING YOURSELF

EMBRACING THE PAST, HOLDING SPACE IN THE NOW AND GROWING TOWARDS THE FUTURE

KAMRYN ROCK

Loving an Honoring Ourselves
Embracing The Past, Holding Space In The Now, And Growing Towards The Future
by Kamryn Rock, Life Coach, CAC 1, CARES CPS-AD
SEL023000 - SELF HELP / Personal Growth / Self-Esteem
SEL045000 - SELF HELP / Journaling
SEL044000- SELF HELP / Self- Management / General
ISBN: 979-8-9880095-0-4(paperback)
ISBN: 979-8-9880095-1-1 (e-book)

Cover design by Ultrakhan22
All images are stock images from Canva and Istock

Printed in the United States of America

Anchored Hearts LLC
P.O. Box 201
Dallas, GA 30132
770-988-4951
www.anchoredheartswellness.com

DEDICATION

Looking back on my life and journey, I can see how every person and event has shaped me and helped me develop into the person I am today. This workbook is dedicated to my beautiful daughter and every perfectly crafted soul that needs a little love and grace. I want to say a quick thank you to my amazing partner (who has always supported me and pushed me to grow), my perfectly imperfect family (who has stood by me every step of the way), and each of my mentors who have continuously poured into me.

TABLE OF CONTENTS

06 — Introduction, how to use this book

07 — Tools and coping skills

09 — The Trauma box

13 — Who am I and why this Jounrey.

14 — The work before the work: Needs

18 — Honoring our body and experiences

30 — How we talk to ourselves

37 — Parts of me

46 — Boundaires

TABLE OF CONTENTS

54

Permission to feel our emotions

69

Dear Me

75

This and That: Yin and Yang

80

The lies we tell ourselves

91

Expectations of ourselves and vulnerability jounral

102

My tank: things that give to me and thinfs that take from me

116

Self care

127

Letter to future self

128

Closing thoughts

129

About the author

HOW TO USE THIS BOOK

Who we are is like a puzzle-every piece has to be there for it to be complete. All of the challenges, triumphs, dark times, pain and joy, tears and laughter-they all make us who we are.

How do I learn to accept, embrace, and honor all of myself and my experiences? I believe in the power of vulnerability and transparency. That being said, I do not have some magical answer to that question. In fact, I am on the journey with you, working through it as I write this all out. Trying to put together some guide or stepping stone for others to join me on the journey of not only discovering who we are, but of learning to love and honor ourselves as well.

I am not a licensed therapist, and this workbook is not meant to be any form of treatment. I do encourage people to make a connection with someone (a therapist, wellness coach, pastor, or whichever path you choose) to provide support through your journey and help you navigate things that may come up for you during this time.

<u>TOOLS</u>

This workbook is solely a guidepost on a journey of discovery we are embarking on together. There may be things that come up for you that may be difficult to face. They may also provide you with an opportunity to grow. I would like to share some tools I have found helpful in times where I may feel a little activated.If you're not familiar with that term let me explain, when I feel activated I may feel an intense emotional reaction, or I may be in a place when my trauma is being triggered or could be triggered on a smaller scale emotionally or mentally.

Breathing. There is plenty of science behind the power of breathing and the impact it has on the brain and body. You can try simple breathing exercises like breathing in for a count of four, holding for a count of four, and then releasing for a count of four.

Yoga. Yoga can help restore your body's natural balance, relieve anxiety, and open energy sources you have stored within you..

Journaling. I have always found journaling a useful tool in my healing journey as it gives me something to look back on, helps me get everything all out, and it brings to light things I may need to discuss with my therapist.

Fidget object. Having a "fidget object", something small you can carry with you like a stone or a ring on your finger that you can spin, can help relieve tension, keep you grounded, and reduce experiences of anxiety.

Meditation and/or somatic mindfulness- the practice of focusing all your attention to the present moment without judgment. This can also help restore balance and peace to your mind and body.

Trauma box
This tool provides a place for you to mentally put up any trauma that may come to the forefront until you are able to meet with a therapist or other treatment provider.

I have personally used all of these tools in my journey and I love each of them. Through this book we will be diving into our needs, our life's experiences, our beliefs, and connecting to our bodies. Buried in all of these things we may uncover some trauma. Trauma can have severe impacts on the body, mind, and emotional well being. I want to introduce and explain the trauma box to make sure it is something that can be used with this workbook to help keep you safe.

What are some other tools you use? If there are any that you have not used but think may be helpful add them here too.

THE TRAUMA BOX

Most of us have experienced some form of trauma in our life. As I mentioned before, this workbook is not therapy, but these exercises may trigger some unexpected feelings within yourself or unlock some stowed away memories. I have found that having what is referred to as a "trauma box" is helpful in those moments. This tool was shared with me by a mentor, Diane Sherman. So I would like you to create your own trauma box in case you need a safe place to stow away negative feelings or experiences until you are able to connect with your support.

Think of a container: what does it look like? Is it a trunk, suitcase or some other form of container? What size is it? Does it have rounded edges or is it sharp? Is it sparkly? Is it matte? What color is it? Does it have pictures on it? Does it have words? Is there a design on it? What does the inside look like? Does it have compartments? Is it padded? Does it have straps inside? Does this container have a lock? If so, who, if anyone, do you want to give a key to? Get as creative and visual as you can with this. The easier it is to see it the easier it is to use it. Remember this is your safe place and you get to determine who has access and how easy or hard it is to access it.

Picture this box and imagine yourself putting it somewhere safe. In the event that something is activated for you in this workbook you can take the box out and safely place the activating event into the box until you are able to connect with your support.

USE THIS PAGE TO CREATE YOUR OWN TRAUMA BOX OR USE THE WORK SHEET ON THE NEXT PAGE

DESIGN AND CREATE YOUR TRAUMA BOX

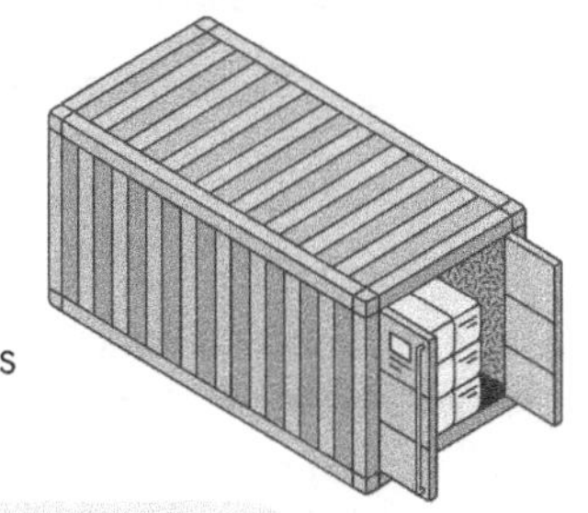

Use this worksheet to help design your box. In the blank spaces add anything you would like

MAIN GOAL

This box you create will be used as a safe place to store anything hard or traumatic that may come up

WHO HAS ACCESS TO THIS BOX?

DESIGNING THE BOX

- [ ] Large
- [ ] Small
- [ ] Rounded edges
- [ ] Sparkly
- [ ] Matte
- [ ] Color
- [ ] Pictures
- [ ] Words

- [ ] Designs
- [ ] Compartments
- [ ] Padded
- [ ] Straps
- [ ] Locked
- [ ] Sharp corned edges
- [ ] Suitcase

- [ ] Box
- [ ] Trunk
- [ ]
- [ ]
- [ ]
- [ ]
- [ ]

- [ ]
- [ ]
- [ ]
- [ ]
- [ ]
- [ ]
- [ ]

DRAW OUT AND COLOR YOUR BOX

MY NOTES

<u>**Who I Am—and Why This Journey?**</u>

As I said earlier, I am a firm believer in vulnerability and transparency. So here we go:

The idea for this workbook was conceived and birthed during one of the hardest times in my life.The past two years my life has shifted and pivoted more times than I can count. Any sense of certainty I had was gone and I had completely lost my sense of self. As I am wading through the muck of an already difficult journey, I tragically lost my younger brother and entered into the hardest grief journey I have ever experienced. I am actively walking this journey, learning how to love and honor myself-all parts of myself-to the best of my ability.

For as long as I can remember, I have struggled with feeling broken and unworthy. I grew up in a home where I experienced a lot of trauma, love, laughter, and pain (more one than the other). I learned to navigate life very early on in ways that weren't meant for me to carry in situations that weren't intended for children. The challenges of those years followed me into my adult life, leading me to face addictions I battled for ten years. As difficult as they were, though, I am grateful for those experiences because they have shaped me and have always taught me something.

<u>THE WORK BEFORE THE WORK: NEEDS</u>

The universe is continuously moving as are we-forward or backwards. I do not believe there is a place of stagnancy. I am either growing and moving forward, or shifting back into old patterns and behaviors.

The year 2020 would be the start of one of the most wild and difficult years and events that I have ever faced (definitely since being sober). I am a busy mother to three amazing children, a partner to my amazing fiancé, active in my family, pursuing a career, an advocate for recovery and mental health-and I was facing some incredible challenges in my life. It is very easy for me to cross my own boundaries and blur the lines between where I end and other things begin. I was not feeling right or like myself. It made me start thinking and really evaluating things, and it hit me: who am I? What do I need?. It had been over four years since I had really sat down to look at what my needs were and who I had become. I had done a good amount of my own work at that point, so I was far from the person I was four years ago. The things I needed then and the things that worked for me then are not working now.

I learned early in my journey of wellness about Maslow's hierarchy of needs and the importance it played in my growth and my relationship with myself. Maslow had a theory that we are constantly working towards self-actualization. He depicts a pyramid with self-actualization at the top and below it on the pyramid basic needs and psychological needs. He believed that we cannot move towards our self-fulfillment needs if our basic and psychological needs are not met. We can also move up and down on the pyramid if things in our lives change.

Let's say we are working on the level of esteem needs, and we lose a job. Now our food, water, warmth, shelter and safety are threatened, so we move back down to the very bottom tier of the pyramid.

Before we can go any further on this journey, we need to pause and identify what our needs are, where we are on the pyramid right now, and evaluate what we need to do to meet those needs before we can move forward. Once we identify our needs, we will take some time to identify how we can ensure our needs are met and how we can meet some of those needs ourselves.

Physiological. The first step is the base of the pyramid-our most basic needs. Some of these include: breathing, food, water, sex, sleep, homeostasis (the balance in the mind and body), and excretion. I would even put medical needs or challenges into this tier.

If these needs are not being met (or we feel like they are not being met) or are being threatened in some way, we can find ourselves in survival mode-or even a state of being physically unwell. When we are in a place of existence in survival mode, it can oftentimes be hard to focus on any other form of growth or look to the future.

Safety. The needs in the second tier include security of the body, employment, resources, morality, family, health, and property. Some of these may include transportation, employment and income, and being free of abuse to name a few. Just as we discussed in the first tier, lack of safety, feeling unsafe, or a threat to these safeties can also put us in a place of survival where we find ourselves and our bodies reactive and not able to focus on growth.

Love/Belonging. The needs discussed here are friendship, family, and sexual intimacy. These can include your biological family, built family, community connection, trusted partner, church, and other forms of fellowships.
Esteem. The fourth tier needs consist of self-esteem, confidence, achievement, respect of others and respect by others. Some things that fit into this category could be working out, attending school, and a respected career to name a few.

Self-actualization. The fifth and final tier of the pyramid consists of morality, creativity, spontaneity, problem-solving, lack of prejudice, and acceptance of facts.

EXERCISE

Draw out your own pyramid and list out your needs for each tier. You can use the space below or use your own material.

Use this page to jot down your needs or to draw your own pyramid.

Maslow's hierarchy of needs

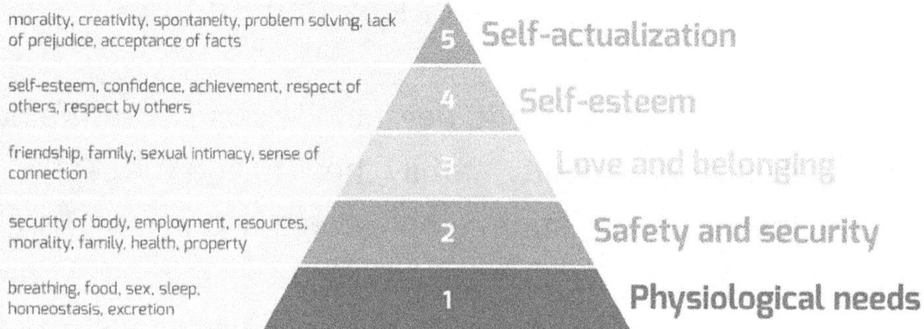

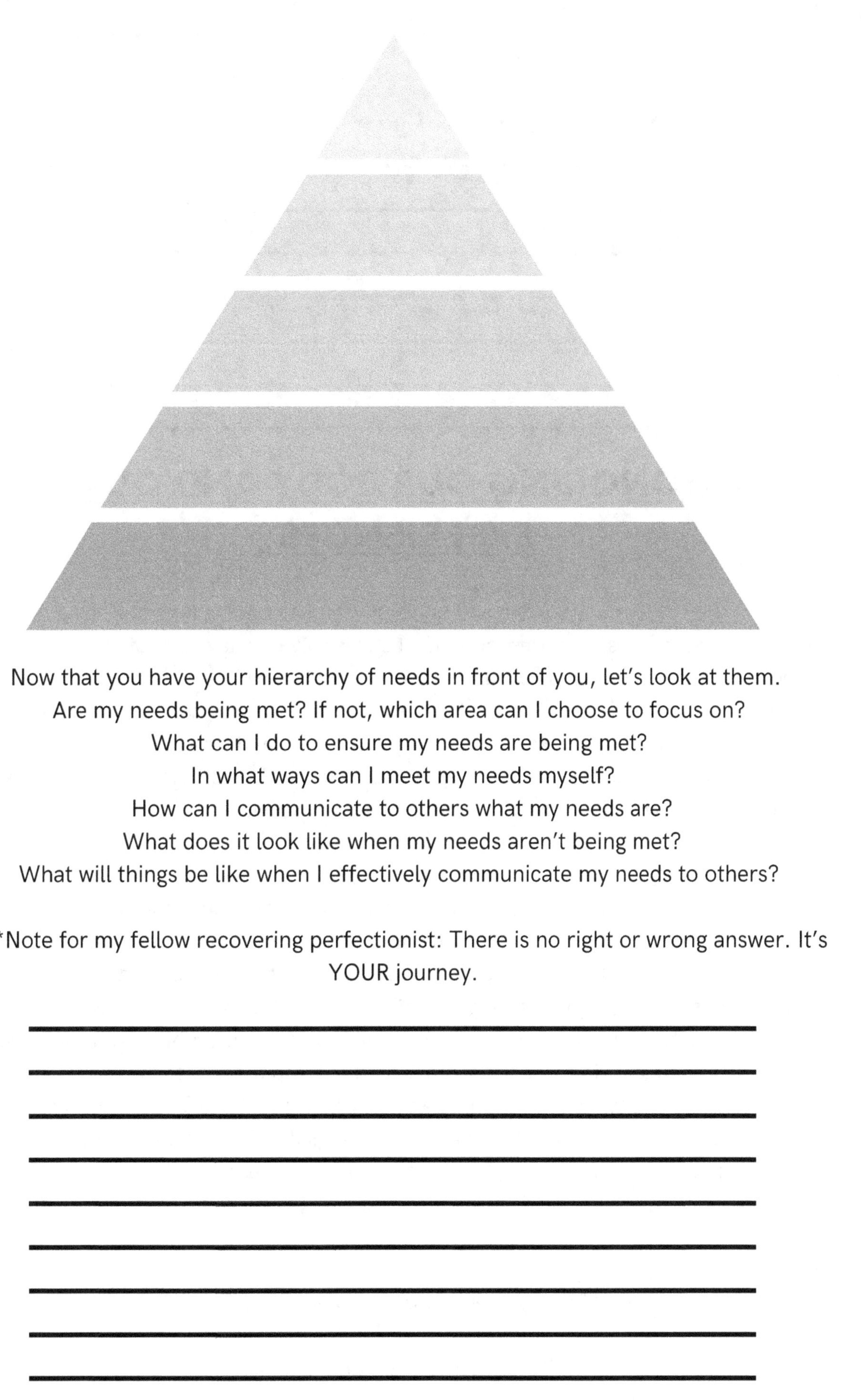

Now that you have your hierarchy of needs in front of you, let's look at them.
Are my needs being met? If not, which area can I choose to focus on?
What can I do to ensure my needs are being met?
In what ways can I meet my needs myself?
How can I communicate to others what my needs are?
What does it look like when my needs aren't being met?
What will things be like when I effectively communicate my needs to others?

***Note for my fellow recovering perfectionist: There is no right or wrong answer. It's YOUR journey.

HONORING OUR BODY AND OUR EXPERIENCES

My journey of learning to love and honor myself has been a long one. One full of pain, fear, challenges, victories, and joy. It still is. My journey has not ended. I do not feel like there is some magical arrival for me and this will be a relationship I get to nurture and grow for the entirety of my physical life. For me, it was not (and sometimes is still not) easy to just jump right in joyous and free loving myself. I spent decades hating myself, judging myself, criticizing myself, just flat out tearing myself to shreds. I would say literally, mentally, and physically beating the shit out of myself everyday.

I don't ever remember a time in my life where I felt beautiful, special, worthy of being loved–hell, even just worthy of being. I constantly compared myself to literally everyone that I felt like was better than me in every way possible and picked out all the reasons I was not good enough. I inflicted a lot of pain and suffering on myself and my body. I have my own relationship with body dysmorphia and disordered eating. I learned later in my journey that I tend to wrap most of my worth up into two things: what my physical body looks like and what I am doing/accomplishing. Each time I had an experience in my life where things didn't work out or I didn't get something I was really hoping for, it deepened that messaging even more. "See, Kamryn? He thinks you're disgusting and no one is ever going to be okay with the way your belly looks."

"See? I knew I was not smart enough."

"I told you you couldn't do this."

So with decades worth of messaging saying I am not good enough, I am not worthy, no one loves me, I can never do great things, I will never be that kind of beautiful, and I will NEVER measure up, how in the hell am I supposed to just start loving myself?

Short answer, I'm not but I can start somewhere. I believe a good place to start is working on honoring my body and myself. Maybe I hate the way my belly looks, but that's okay. An old scar reminds me I almost died at ten days old... but I am here! I have created and birthed two amazing beings, and I have the stretch marks and scars to prove it. One of those scars reminds me that I almost lost my firstborn, that she had to be delivered via emergency cesarean, and that I was told I was lucky to have her and would never have another child. The other scar, well, that one is from my beautiful baby boy–the baby boy that came after my daughter.

Maybe I don't like the way my belly looks, but look at the fucking amazing things it has done! Maybe I have big feet with calluses. Those feet brought me through hell and back. My toes curl a little and it bothers me. I believe it is from the years I wore shoes that didn't fit quite right because I wanted to have cool things but we didn't have money so I took what I could. I don't love the curl in my toes, but I can 100% honor and love the little girl who grew into them. My thighs and arms are covered in scars from self-harm, and in the summer you can see the marks a little more clearly than in other times of the year. I don't love them, but I can honor my strong legs and arms for all they have done. I can honor the fact that I have grown so much in my life that I no longer feel the need to self-harm. I can also honor the little girl who felt like that was all she had.

I have a tendency to be a little naturally reactive, hyper-vigilant and I over function. I recognize now that it does not serve me and can often be more hurtful than helpful. Those things literally kept me alive long ago. There is a multitude of positive and negative feelings, thoughts, and beliefs I carry about my body and my experiences. Even with the ebb and flow of those things I can look at basic facts and I can honor myself and my body in general for making it through every single day I have lived so far. I can honor my body for fighting off sickness, for moving when I needed it to, for still working for me when I hated and abused it.

Write out a letter or some points to your body below in all the ways that it has served you and how you honor it and appreciate it, we can just start there.

For a seed to grow it's placed in absolute darkness and dirt. When we break an arm or we become sick our body needs to be still and rest. Sometimes to replenish crops and fields someone will set fire to them and let it burn. Places that experience severe droughts praise the storm. The trees die every year and experience new growth. Everything I have been through, all that I have experienced: good and bad, can have a purpose and be useful.

What fires have you been burned by?

How can this fire be helpful?

What things did the fire extinguish in your life?

What was able to grow from the fire?

What dark have you experienced in your life?

What can you do with that dark?

What was able to take root in that darkness?

What light was on the other side of that darkness?

We have all experienced difficult things in life and events that have transformed us in one way or another. Thinking about your life and experiences, what useful things are you filled with? How can these things be helpful?

What has needing taught you?

How can you listen to your body?

What things do you give to yourself?

How can you practice giving to yourself?

Is there an empty place in you? What is this place: describe it,
where is it? What does it look like? What does it feel like?

____

____

____

____

____

____

____

____

____

____

____

____

____

What can you now plant in that empty place?

____

____

____

____

____

____

____

MY NOTES

MY NOTES

<u>How We Talk To Ourselves</u>

When I was in residential treatment, we worked a lot on affirmations and the way that we talked to ourselves. It can take a lot of effort-and I mean a real conscious effort-to retrain our thoughts and change the things we say to ourselves.

Do you have someone that really gets under your skin or that you really dislike? What are some of the thoughts you have when you see them or hear their name?

"Ugh here we go again, I cannot stand them."
"Why is he so stupid and full of himself?"
"Can she not find someone else to bother?"

How do you behave towards them? How does your body react? You may avoid them, you might feel some type of anger or aggression in your body, you may get tense, you may just find yourself in a bad mood just having to deal with them, right?
My point here is this: thoughts become things. How we think about things determines how we feel about them, which then can impact how we behave.
If our thoughts about ourselves are shit, we are going to feel like shit about ourselves and treat ourselves like shit!
During my experience in treatment, I had this affirmation taped on my mirror:

Be careful how you talk to yourself;
you're always listening

This paper is still taped to my mirror in my bathroom. It has helped me so many times by reminding me to slow down and pay attention to the things I am saying to myself.

We have thousands of thoughts a day, many of those being ones I would call unconscious thoughts. It takes time to be able to change those thoughts. It does not mean we will not have them, but we may be able to catch and change them sooner.

One thing that I have found useful in my journey is listening to motivational speakers. One of my favorites is Lisa Nichols. If you have never listened to her, I would strongly recommend it.

One of the things I carry with me from her is an activity in which you stand in front of a mirror, look yourself in the eye, then say the following statements (completing each sentence with your own personal declaration):

I am proud that you…..

I forgive you for….

I commit to you that……

I found it empowering to add a couple more for myself:

I love your………

I give you permission to…..

You can do the same. Feel free to add anything your soul may need.

I would suggest doing these exercises for thirty days, but I personally know how hard that may be sometimes. So shoot instead for seven days, and when you finish those seven days, try for seven more. I have also provided space below for you to journal the experience and note anything that comes up during the process.

Each day, try and say something different than the day before. I found it helpful to write them on my mirror with a marker.

Triangle of Self-Talk

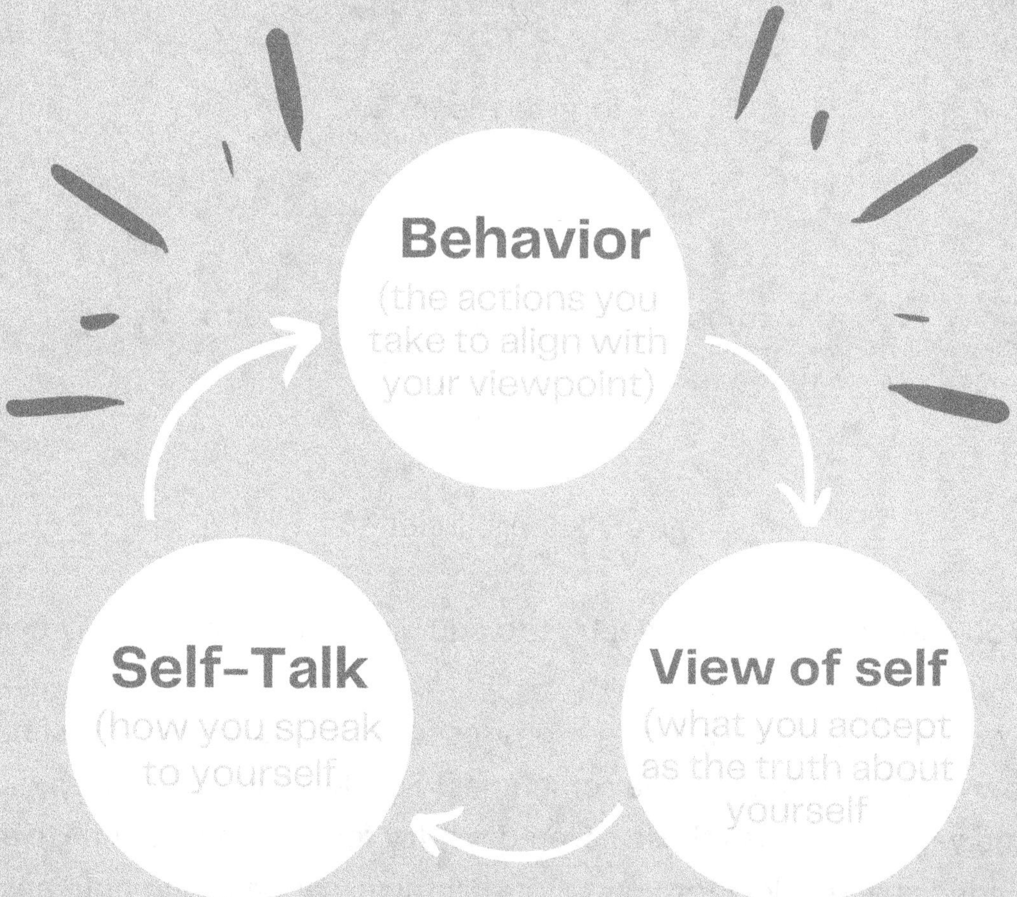

Were there things that were hard to say or hear?

What is this telling you?

What was this experience like? Is it getting easier?

____

____

____

____

____

____

____

____

Becoming more aware of our thoughts can be challenging. Most of our thoughts are automatic, unconscious and can come from deeply ingrained beliefs about ourselves. We may not initially know what thoughts we had about ourselves throughout the day. If you are struggling with identifying these thoughts I think a step towards being able to do that is to start by looking at experiences we may have throughout the day and trying to trace that back to a thought we may be having about ourselves. I will give you some examples from my personal life and real-life situations.

Example

At the end of a busy day, my partner asks me if I got the laundry put away. I find myself full of rage-my body gets hot, my thoughts start racing, and I snap. WHOA! What just happened? All he did was ask me a simple question, the answer to which is no. Simple as that, but here is what happened in my head:

I did not get the laundry up because I am a terrible partner and cannot keep up with my house and family. I am a piece of shit.

So I find myself reactive because of the messaging I am feeding myself.

When I first got custody of my daughter back, it was a challenge for both of us. There were countless nights that she cried, and just as many nights that I felt didn't go as planned. After I would finally get her to bed and my partner would try and have a conversation with me, I would be extremely short, irritated and snappy. Why was I feeling so aggressive and angry? What was going on?

Here was the messaging in my head:

I feel like she hates me. I don't know what I am doing. I am a terrible mom. She was better off where she was before she came back to me.

There was one time that I had a late meeting, and when I got home I discovered that my family had already eaten and had not gotten anything for me.

"You didn't get me anything?"

"No, I thought you ate."

I immediately shut down and my responses became those like, "No, I'm good." I wasn't even hungry so what did it matter?

What was going through my head was that they hadn't even called me, what I wanted didn't matter, no one cared about me, I didn't matter.

My point is that sometimes we can trace an event or behavior back to a feeling and a thought. This may be helpful in identifying the thoughts you're having about yourself, as well as some patterns in those thoughts

Exercise: Recall some events from the past few days or weeks, then try to trace back to thoughts about yourself:

What thoughts did you identify? If they were loving and positive, no need to change them. If they were not, how can you correct or replace them?

Over the next thirty days (or seven if the thought of thirty is overwhelming), catch and change those negative thoughts. Speak to yourself in the same way you speak to someone you love. Speak to yourself in a way that ignites passion, fuels you, and builds you up. Even if you do not believe it now, I want you to keep practicing it.

<u>PARTS OF ME</u>

Starting my journey of wellness and recovery was tough. On the one hand, there was the person I had become over the years, and on the other hand, there was the person I was becoming. There were times I felt so conflicted because there were still parts of the old me that I felt weren't supposed to follow me on my journey into becoming the new me. Were these things still acceptable?

I had the same feelings and thoughts when I began my professional journey. I was trying to define who I was as an addiction counselor, a helping professional, and an advocate for recovery. I had expectations of who I was supposed to be and what was "appropriate ".
These same feelings of conflict popped up in my role as a mom. I would often feel "wrong" or out of place. I would feel "not like myself".
What does a good mother do? How does she behave? Are these parts of me okay? What I have learned for myself is that they are all okay. They are all parts of me, and that is just fine.
I often would feel like a fraud or like there was something wrong with me. What I noticed in this instance was that it was coming from this incongruence of who I am and what I felt like I was supposed to be. Let me explain, I had this preconceived notion that a helping professional was this be all end all, perfect, put together person and that wasn't me. I had this belief that as a mom I was "supposed" to parent a certain way, look put together, and not make mildly inappropriate comments. So when I tried to be these things I thought I needed to be I felt like an imposter and internally miserable. I was trying to hide and suffocate parts of me that I believed were not acceptable.

We have all these parts of us, and in the center is our highest self, our best self. On the other side we have other parts of us. Maybe we have this part of us that is really angry, intolerant, impatient and disconnected. Some days we may have this part of us show up that is super insecure, makes you feel really small, inferior and doesn't use our voice. There can be parts of us that may be super promiscuous, validation seeking, co-dependent, or even manipulative. I think when we are able to define these parts of us- then name, understand, and embrace them--it is easier for us to love and honor all of who we are. I can be a helping professional and still seek my own support. I can be understanding and compassionate and still get angry. I can be a good mom and still embrace my wilder side. I can be professional and still mildly inappropriate while rocking my little shorts. It's ok if have this part of me that is super intolerant, angry, disconnected, and judgmental. If I can identify it, name it, notice when that part shows up, take note of why it shows up and understand what that part of me is feeling and needing then I can co-exist and work with that part of me. When I am able to understand and embrace that part of me I can use pieces of it when needed and not have to allow it to consume me.

Let's get to it! What are these parts of us? Take some time and create these parts of you. Who is it? What is the name of this part? What does this part look like? What are the characteristics ? What triggers this part? When does it show up? When do you need it to show up? When do you need it to stay behind? How does it serve you? What ways
can it get in the way? Use the next few pages to create these parts.

Use the next few pages to create the parts of you. Get as specific and creative as you can. If you need more pages feel free to use your own journal. Don't forget to create your best self, your highest self and what that looks like.

<u>BOUNDARIES</u>

When I say I had no boundaries when I started this journey, I mean I had, like, zero boundaries. It was hard for me to have them; I literally did not care about or like myself at all. I had little to no insight into who I was, what I needed, what I really stood for, what impacted me negatively, or what I was not willing to participate in.

An important piece of loving and honoring ourselves is knowing and setting our personal boundaries, as well as upholding them with ourselves, others, and the world around us. It also means knowing where we end and others begin.

We can have boundaries with our family, ourselves, friends, co-workers, and our intimate relationship partners. Our boundaries can be different with different groups. A boundary I have with my family, for example, won't be the same boundary I have with a co-worker. Something I am willing to accept from–or even discuss with–an intimate partner is not necessarily something I would be willing to accept or discuss with a family member.

I struggled so much with codependency , unhealthy boundaries, over functioning and burning myself out, and enmeshment with others that I oftentimes did not know where I ended and others began. It was hard for me to distinguish what was mine to carry and what was not.
If you struggle with the idea of boundaries or have a hard time identifying what yours are, it's okay. You are not alone! We can start with your absolutes. These are our hard No's. The things that we absolutely will not tolerate, participate in, or do not want.

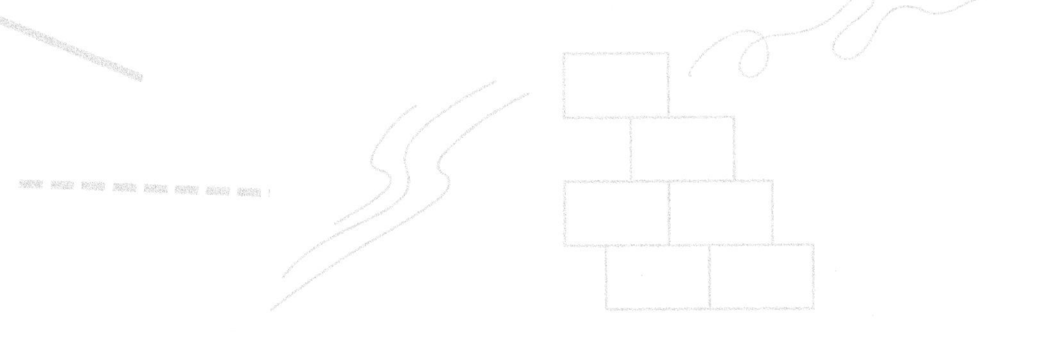

Take a few minutes and identify some of the groups or relationships in your life and what the absolutes are for these people. For example, an absolute for a romantic relationship would be cheating, or an absolute for a work environment could be acts of discrimination or racism.

Now that we have some absolutes and the thoughts are flowing, let's define some specific boundaries. It's okay if these aren't actually in place yet. You can use this space to begin developing them now.

Have you ever had someone cross a boundary you had?

What was that like for you? Were you able to uphold the boundary?

What was difficult about the situation? What do you think you did well in
the situation?

Jot down your thoughts on how boundaries can help love and honor yourself.

Use the space below (or your own space) to create an image of what your boundaries look like today? Create another image that depicts what you would like them to look like in the future

How do you think your life may change with these boundaries? How would you feel?

What would you do or not do? What would you start to do?

How would you act?

How would people respond to you?

____

____

____

____

____

____

____

____

____

What steps can you take today to start making the changes with your boundaries

____

____

____

____

____

____

____

____

____

Permission to Feel Our Emotions

I am a sucker for a good kids' movie, even at my age. Of my hundreds of favorites is "Inside Out". I think it is crucial to teach our children, or people in general, the value in each of our emotions and the importance of feeling them freely (all of them).

The movie starts out with the main character, a little girl named Riley, experiencing the emotion of Joy. As she gets older and things happen in her life, other emotions are introduced: anger, fear, disgust and sadness. Through the plot of the movie, the joy emotion realizes that sadness is just as important.

Growing up in my home, I was hyper aware of the following emotions: happiness, fear, sadness, and anger. Anger became my main default.

Most people can name a handful of emotions but studies have shown there are 27 emotions and that humans can experience 34,000 emotions. The eight foundations for all other emotions are joy, sadness, acceptance, disgust, fear, anger, anticipation and surprise.

If we are taught and given permission to feel and express very few emotions, what do we do with the rest of them, and how does that impact us? Did we learn how to process through them and manage them? Did we feel loved and supported through all of the emotions?

I believe our society, in general, is one of "pull yourself together and keep it moving." Just keep moving and doing, fake it till you make it.

Have you ever experienced something tragic and felt hesitance from people around you to ask how you were doing? It's like they believe you are contagious, and that your sadness will somehow get on them. Note their uncomfortable squirm when you have the courage to say you are suffering or experiencing excruciating grief.

There are those of us who may never have learned about the emotions under the foundational section of anger. Everything may come out as anger. Sadness may be expressed as anger because sad wasn't something we were allowed to be. When we limit our emotions, we limit our world and our capacity to grow and connect. We diminish our potential and our ability to live and love to the fullest. When I was in treatment and they had us work on identifying emotions, I would often have to stare at the feelings wheel for quite some time before I was able to connect and identify with an emotion. If we haven't been taught about emotions, given permission to feel them, a safe place to experience them, and tools to manage them, it can be difficult to even identify what we are feeling. We can also feel "wrong" or "bad" for feeling an emotion if we weren't provided the space to explore and experience a particular emotion.

I recently watched Brene Brown's "Atlas of the Heart" (which I also highly recommend). In it, she talks about the importance of naming our emotions by the right name and calling them what they really are. The thing about our brain and body is that they will always do what they are told. If you call it anger, you will feel and experience anger.
An example that happens often in my house is with my kids. When they choose not to listen, I can get angry. I have angry thoughts. I tell myself I am angry. I have an angry voice and angry behavior. When I am able to practice the pause, step back, and actually name the emotion and behave accordingly, it is not the same.

Sometimes they choose not to help me, and I may feel frustrated or aggravated, which feels different than full blown anger. Sometimes I dissect it a little further. (Note: please keep in mind that this is my experience. I am not saying this is true for everyone, but I am positive someone can relate.) When my kids choose not to do something that I ask of them, I may feel angry. What can be behind that anger feeling is actually fear-fear that I am losing control of the messaging and belief that I am not a good mom.

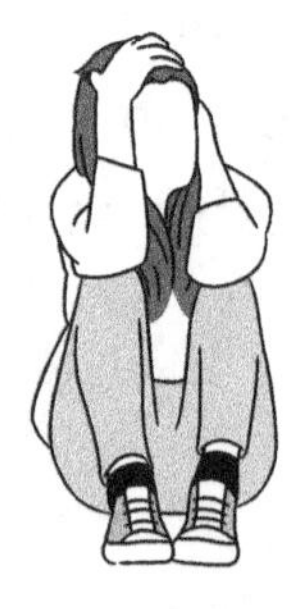

I may have unrealistic expectations of myself as a mom. I may even have unrealistic expectations of my children, believing that they will always make good choices. You see how giving yourself permission to feel all of the emotions and naming them correctly can make a huge difference.

When it comes to learning, feeling, and managing emotions, it's often drawn from social experiences, both spoken and unspoken. We can learn about this in our families, society, culture, and environment.

Where did you learn about emotions?

What messages were you given about emotions?

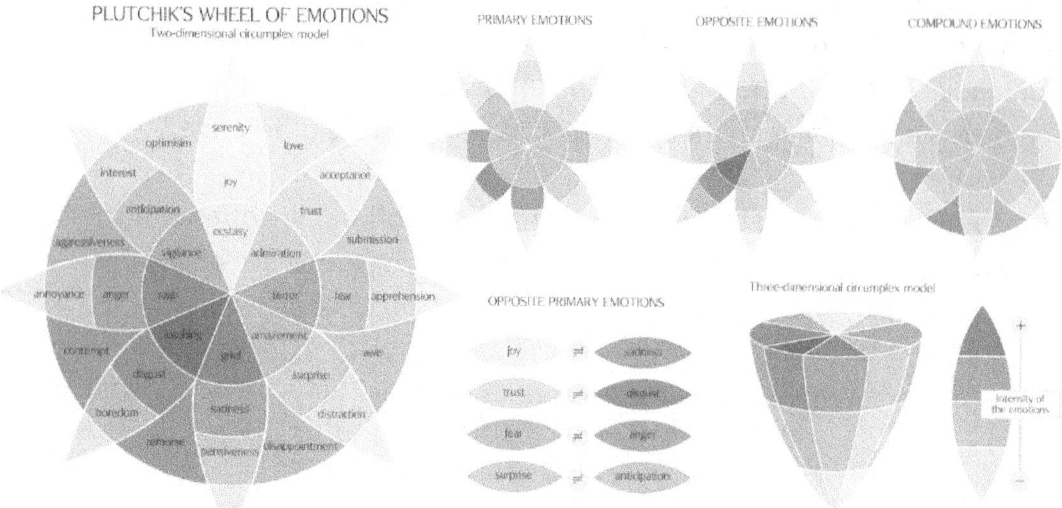

I am going to list some other emotions below. I do not want you to limit yourself to what is on the wheel. There may be emotions and feelings you have never considered or been able to actually name.

When going through this exercise also consider these but note this is not a be-all-end-all list, and if you come up with others, feel free to use them:

Despair, tunnned, hostile, hate, longing, passion, peaceful, helpless, satisfied, blissful, stimulated, neglected, affectionate, infatuated, relieved, hysterical, mortified, panic, nervous, annoyed, hurt, suffering, guilty, shameful, dismayed, speechless, overcome, amused, awe-struck, hopeful, enchanted, inferior, inadequate, envy, sorrow, proud, delighted, optimistic, pessimistic, euphoric, sentimental, to name a few.

What emotions on the wheel do you identify the most with?

Are there emotions on the wheel that make you uncomfortable or that you
have a challenging time giving yourself permission to feel?

____

____

____

____

____

____

____

Do you feel like you misname your emotions? If so, how does that impact you
and your life?

____

____

____

____

____

____

Over the next week spend some time with the feeling wheel. Be mindful of how you are feeling. Use the space below as a feelings journal. Jot down what you felt for the day. How did you feel in your body? Did you feel conflicted about feeling the emotion? Did it feel weird or natural?
How did you give yourself permission and space to feel the emotion? What were you telling yourself? How do you feel you managed the emotion? How can feeling this emotion be helpful in your life?

What have you noticed that shifted? How can you continue to make
positive changes in this area?

my notes

my notes

<u>**Dear Me**</u>

"If I knew then what I know now…"

I've heard it a million times. We can look at that saying as the basis of the next exercise in our journey.

I feel like there are so many things I needed to know and hear through my life that I didn't always get. There is always some part of us in there that is still longing to hear the things we needed to hear. Some part of us that is filled with shame for not being understood or forgiven. There may be parts of us that feel as though we will never be good enough, some parts of us that desperately need to be given permission to release it, to own it, to love ourselves, and to be proud of who we are.

I have mentioned meditation several times now, and I believe it can be used for many things. For the first part of the activity, we are going to start with a meditation that will help get us to a place where we can freely participate in the second part of the activity. I know it may be hard for some of us to read, remember, and follow a meditation on paper, and that's okay. We don't need to follow it perfectly, though it may be helpful to read through it a time or two and then try.
Start by getting into a comfortable position laying down or sitting. Close your eyes and relax

Feel your body loosen and start to sink into the surface you are sitting or laying on.

Focus on your breath. Breathe in slowly, feel the air filling your lungs, and breathe out. Spend a few minutes here breathing in and out, sending your breath to each part of you body, imagining your breath as a golden light. As you breathe in, picture this golden light filling your body.

Imagine standing at the top of a staircase. Feel your bare feet on the stairs. You start walking down the staircase. There is enough light to see just the next step. You count down the stairs from the top:

15...14...13...12...11...10...9...8...7...6...5...4...3...2...1...

You reach the bottom.

At the bottom, you see a door and just enough light shining through it to illuminate the door frame. It's a big oak wood door with a brass knob. You open the door and walk into a field. You feel the sunshine on your skin, see the flowers and the tall grass. Smell the clean air. You step out into the field and feel the ground beneath your bare feet.
Open your arms wide, take in the sun and breathe in the golden light. You're breathing in and out, paying attention to each breath and sending the light to each part of your body.

In the distance, standing at the edge of a lake being filled by a waterfall, you see a child. As you walk closer to the child, you notice that the child is you. How old are you? What do you look like? How does little you want to embrace? Does little you say anything?
Spend some time with yourself. Take little you by the hand and walk into the lake until you are both submerged. Staying hand in hand, turn around together and start to return and as you are coming back out of the water, see the light getting brighter as you breach the surface of the water. As you both stand to walk back to shore, feel all the water roll off your body. Rolling off your head, down your shoulders and arms. All the water runs down your upper body to your legs and your feet, leaving a puddle where you stand. You both step out of the puddle feeling the sun dry your clothes.
Say your goodbyes to little you. Walk back to the big oak door across the field. Grab the brass door knob and walk back up the stairs with enough light to see the next step, counting each step:
1...2...3...4...5...6...7...8...9...10...11...12...13...14...15...
As you reach the top, take a deep breath. Slowly inhale. And exhale. When you are ready, open your eyes and come back to the room.

When you are ready, use the space below-or your journal-to write a
letter to your younger self, at whatever age or period in your life you
would like to address.

<u>**This and That:
Yin and Yang**</u>

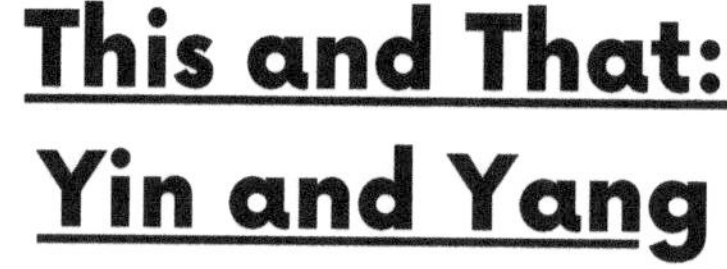

My world stopped at 6:00 PM January 25th 2022.

Losing my little brother was and still is the hardest thing I have ever walked through. I have spent time in my studies learning about grief, facilitating groups on grief, and even helping others walk through their grief, but this just hit differently. I was experiencing grief in a way I never had before.

I found myself in this place of not allowing myself to feel joy or continue to move forward. Even with what I had previously learned about grief, there still seemed to be this subconscious internal messaging: How can I be so hurt and smile? How can I miss my brother this much and laugh? How could I have just experienced this tragedy and still want so much for myself? These two opposite can't exist, can they?

I thought about this often and wondered where else it might show up in my life. It dawned on me how black and white my thinking or internal messages could still be. I had this all or nothing, in or out idea system in so many areas of my life. How some part of me struggled to embrace the dualities of life. I started to see it in all areas of my life. I realized I can be a good mom and not handle every situation as I would like to. I can struggle with the way I feel about my body and still love myself. I can take a break from school and still be driven. I can experience my own struggle and be a good mentor. I can have days that I am in a space of reaction and still be a good partner. I can be devastated by a loss and still enjoy my life.

I often think we do this to ourselves without even being aware of it. I started to think about how this incongruence impacted me. What would it be like if I wasn't constantly battling myself trying to prove some twisted point? I can't love myself because I hate my stomach. I just lost my best friend-how dare I live my life! I yelled at my kids today, so I am a terrible mother. I'm just always angry, they deserve better. What would it be like if I allowed myself to embrace the duality in the existence of these things together?

Can you think of areas in your life that you can see the same thing? What are they for you?

If you went to bed tonight and woke the next morning to find this and that existing together, what would it be like? How would you feel? Would your life be different? Would your relationship with yourself and others be different ? In what ways would things be different ?

NOTES

NOTES

The Lies We Tell Ourselves

When we are created, before we are birthed into this world, we are our own beings, a blank canvas, if you will. We come into this world with no preconceived notions or perceptions. We are born naked with no shame for our body. When we are that chunky little baby, everyone celebrates and loves our little rolls. When learning to walk, we fall and do not judge this as failure or criticize ourselves.

When we are school-aged and learning to write our names, we are celebrated for the small victories of growth and progress. We are wild, free, curious, loving, loud, and full of big emotions.

As we grow into adolescence and young adulthood, the world wears us down as we learn about it from everything around us. We carry the beliefs of our friends, family, and society. We learn what we are supposed to look like, who we are supposed to be, how we should act, how success is measured, and what is important. We change ourselves, we adapt, we become things that may not match who we are internally. Don't get me wrong-we can learn a lot of valuable things and carry important messaging with us pertaining to values, kindness, emotional intelligence, right and wrong, and morals.

I am willing to put money on the fact that the majority of us are carrying around messaging that does not belong to us. Things that do not make us feel well. Things that make us feel internally bad about ourselves. Many of us carry beliefs from experiences in our childhood that are conflicting and cause us to feel worthless. These unconscious or conscious beliefs can lead to unrealistic expectations that make us feel we can never measure up.

In a world of constant comparisons, it can be helpful to look at what we are carrying. Are these things true? Where did I get these beliefs from? Do they serve me? Do I want to continue to carry this with me? How does it impact my life? What, instead, is actually true?

I carried a lot of messaging with me that I was not even aware of for a very long time. These beliefs caused me to act in certain ways that were not helpful for me and, instead, perpetuated the cycle of the belief. Our brains have the need to be right, so when we believe things deeply, we will act in a manner that will cause the event to happen, to prove ourselves right.

When we believe that we are unlovable and everyone will leave us, we may act in ways that will push people away so our brain can say, "See? I told you. No one loves you. Everyone leaves."

These beliefs came from somewhere, though not necessarily ever spoken directly to you. Your parents may have been divorced, your grandparents passed, your best friend moved away, and your favorite teacher leaves. As a child, the way you process this could be that everyone you love leaves-and it's your fault.

We are connectional beings, and our tendency leans towards needing things to make sense. It can be difficult for us, especially as children, to just let life happen as it does without judgment, fault, shame, or blame.
I have picked up a belief that if I don't look a certain way, then I am not pretty-I am disgusting and unworthy. I have a belief that I cannot lose weight.

I carry a belief that if I am not doing great things, making strides, and accomplishing amazing feats, then I am not good enough. That I am unworthy and have no purpose. I carried a belief for a long time that I was unlovable and that people I care about leave me.

I have a belief and unrealistic expectation of "perfect" parenting-that if I am not meeting that, then I am not being a good mom.

I fight with beliefs about success. It is hard for me to believe I can be successful and prosperous.

I didn't grow up with much, so I fear not having enough. Poverty as a child causes me to struggle now with believing I am capable of making and managing money.

The mind is a powerful thing, and life is about perception and beliefs. What we believe is true to us. If we believe we can, we can. If we believe we cannot, then we cannot. If we believe we are something, then we are. If we believe we are not, then we are not.

I think it's easy to see how these beliefs can impact my life, my relationships with people, myself, my work, and my happiness.

I would encourage you to take some time and write out the conscious or unconscious beliefs you carry. What are the lies you tell yourself?

____

____

____

____

____

____

____

____

____

____

____

____

What experiences shaped these beliefs?

Do these beliefs belong to someone else?

How do these impact your life? How do they show up in your progress,
your relationships, your finances, every area of your life?

Are these things that serve you? Are they things you would like to let go of?

One of the great things about being human is the power of our mind and the ability to change it. I used to believe I was not good in school, but I changed my belief to a growth mindset, which allowed me to feel capable of learning and growing. I ended up in the honor society in my first year of college.

With your messages and beliefs in mind, which of these could be true instead? What can we change them to that will help us achieve wellness and the life we deserve? What is the actual truth?

____

____

____

____

____

____

____

____

____

____

____

____

____

Notes

Notes

Expectations of Ourselves and Vulnerability Journal

We all have expectations of ourselves and the world around us. Expectations of how things should go, how people should act and behave, what life is "supposed" to look like. These expectations are formed over time. We are not born with them. We develop them through experiences and messages we learn from those around us. Oftentimes these expectations can be from and intertwined with our beliefs.

In my case, I have found that I can have a lot of unrealistic expectations that put me in a place of fear-based living focused on control. These expectations can also set me up for internal conflict and disappointment. Not all expectations are negative or harmful. Many of them serve to help us develop values and boundaries. They can help us develop healthy relationships and steer us away from ones that do not serve us.

As an example, let's use an unrealistic expectation of mine that is not based in healthy living and does not serve me in any way: what my body "should" look like. I have this picture in my head of an amazing lean, toned, ab-defined flat stomach. A perfect figure and tan. It's okay to want those

things, and I am continuing to work on my journey of health. But here is the reality:

I have had two c-sections and one surgery, so my stomach may never look like that without a surgical procedure.

And here is where the problematic messaging and beliefs come in:

If I do not look like that, then my partner will not find me attractive and will leave.

Now let's go deeper: if that is the case, then what?

Then he will leave. Then that means I am not worthy. Then that means I may be alone forever.

Another unrealistic expectation for me is aspiring to be the "perfect" parent. Here is the reality:

I am human and perfection is not possible.

Here is the flawed messaging and belief:

If I am not the perfect parent then my kids will experience pain or not have what they need.

If that is the case, then what?
Then that means I failed. Then that means I am worthless.

I also have this unrealistic expectation that I can carry it all, help everyone, get every task completed, and be superwoman. If I can't (which I cannot because I am human and have boundaries), then I have failed. Which means people won't need, like, or value me. Then what? Then I am alone and worthless.

Do you see a pattern here? These are just a few of my unrealistic expectations—there are many more. I am sure you can relate somehow to these scenarios.

I want you to get vulnerable with yourself and go through the process of looking at your own expectations. Look at the beliefs behind them. Where do they come from? What are you afraid of?

These may be hard to identify in one sitting, so over the next few days or weeks, take some time to be an observer in your life. If you are having trouble identifying these things, you can start by looking at your behavior. Remember before when I said all behavior is goal-oriented. There is a reason we do things.

Apply the If...Then process in my examples to your own expectations. Remember that whatever comes to mind comes there for a reason. It can be important, or it can even be as simple as this: parking in front of people can make me anxious. Why? Because if I make a mistake parking, I am an idiot, a failure. People won't like me or they will judge me. If they judge me they may think I am unworthy or less than.

After looking at our expectations-and I mean the unrealistic ones that cause more harm than good- think about freeing yourself from them to allow for more realistic and loving expectations. If you found a genie lamp and were granted the ability to free yourself from these ties what would you feel like?

What would you be able to let go of? What would you be able to do?

How would you dress? What would work or school look like?

How would your relationships be different? How would the relationship with yourself be different ?

NOTES

NOTES

<u>My Tank:
Things That Give to Me...and Things That Take From Me</u>

Now that we have been able to do a little root work to look at who we are and develop a little compassion and care for ourselves, I think it will be a little easier to look at valuing ourselves, our energy, and taking care of ourselves.

This particular exercise was shared with me by another mentor of mine, Marc Pimsler. When doing this exercise, let's think of ourselves as being a gas tank-only we will call it an energy tank. Everything in our life either gives us something that fills our energy tank, or uses energy that takes away from our tank. In my life, for instance, these things can be my kids, my work, and my sponsees.

If we are aware of exactly what is coming in and what is going out, it can make it easier to give ourselves a little grace and compassion when we aren't functioning at one hundred percent.

Use the space below (or your own paper) and draw yourself-a stick person is totally okay. From this person, draw arrows going in (for everything that feeds you or gives to you) and arrows going out (for everything that depletes or takes away your energy). Remember that some things in our lives can do both.

Looking at the picture in its entirety, can you see if there is anything you would like to adjust? Is there balance in what is going in and what is going out? Is there anything you need to add or take away?

Spend some time over the next few days evaluating your "tank" and how much energy you have put out. Each morning when you get up, take a scan of your body and your mind. How full is your tank? Are you at 100% today? Or maybe you only have 45% today. Either way is okay, but knowing where you are at the start will make it easier to determine how best to use the energy you do have in prioritizing your day.

Maybe a project needs to get done today, but the laundry can wait till tomorrow, for example. Or time at the park with the kids is a must for you and them, but pizza is okay for dinner tonight.

Use the space below as a journal to jot down thoughts, patterns, and ideas over the next seven days. Each morning and evening, evaluate where your tank is. Is there something you can adjust? Is it hard for you to give yourself the grace to be at 45%? How does it feel when you're at 100%? What does it take for you to be at 100%? Is there anything you can add to feed yourself and keep you operating at a higher frequency?

Day 1:

____

____

____

____

____

____

____

____

____

____

____

____

____

____

____

____

____

Day 2:

Day 3:

Day 4:

Day 5:

Day 6:

Day 7:

After these seven days has anything shifted for you?

Thinking back to before Day 1 and at the end of Day 7, is there anything you have started to do differently?

Were there any patterns that emerged?

How does it feel to value yourself and your energy?

<u>Self-Care</u>

Self-care is what I would call the maintenance of this journey. We have worked on learning to love and honor ourselves so that now, hopefully, taking care of ourselves is an expectation and a must. We have learned to value and love who we are, and now it's time to show that love on a daily basis. Yes DAILY! We are going to make sure we are giving to ourselves, filling that tank.

I am a do-er of all things, and I will go, go, go till there is no more go. Time and time again, I have run until my tank was depleted and there was nothing left to give. Not to me, my kids, my family, or friends. If I am not taking care of myself, what I put out is not wholehearted connection. It's not purpose-filled work. It's not intentional. It's typically coming from a place of survival because I have nothing left to give.

As a mom, a partner, and an over-functioner, it was hard for me to grasp that I have to take care of me first (over the years, the universe and my higher power have made it clear that I have to), but the lesson came up again and again until I was ready to accept it. I also had to learn exactly what self-care looked like and meant for me specifically at any given moment, whether I am at 45% or 80%.

I think that we sometimes culturally develop beliefs about self-care. We live in a society where business is praised and your level of exhaustion equals the level of your success. The more you have going on, the better you are. It can be hard for us to understand that slowing down and taking care of ourselves is a must. It's just like a car-it may go for a while, but if you continue to run on "E" with low oil and the engine light on, at some point it's going to give out!

What are your thoughts and beliefs about self-care?

____

____

____

____

____

____

____

____

____

____

____

____

____

____

____

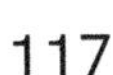

Where did you learn these beliefs about self-care?

How do you define self care? What things do you consider self care?

____

____

____

____

____

____

____

____

____

____

____

____

____

____

Jot down a few things you do for self-care. If you don't do it yet, that is okay. Write instead some things you think you may enjoy or that may help you.

In a typical week, how would you rate your self-care practice? From 0 (being none) to 10 (being its an absolute must and I practice it very well)

____

____

____

What challenges do you face with your self-care, or what are some areas for growth?

____

____

____

____

____

____

____

____

____

____

____

What do you do well in your self-care practice?

Self-care does not have to be complicated. It can vary greatly depending on the person or situations. It doesn't have to be hours-long or costly. Self-care may simply be:

Upholding boundaries and valuing your time and energy (it's okay to say no)

Getting your nails or hair done

Spending time taking a mindful walk

Working out, moving your body

Candlelight baths

Eating for wellness

Taking prescribed medications to help you stay well

Church and spiritual connection

Taking yourself to lunch

Meditation

Yoga

Reading

Scheduled kid-free time

Participating in a hobby you like

Good sleep habits

Healthy connection

Meetings or fellowship connection

Connecting with mentors

Therapy

Spending time in nature
Quiet time alone
Journaling or reflective writing
Spending some time grounding

There are just as many ways to practice self-care that do not cost a thing. Think of self-care as things that give to you and things you do to keep you well.

Is there anything you would like to add to your self care practice?

In this space, let's talk about commitment. For me, life can get extremely busy pretty fast, and if I don't schedule it–it won't happen. It can be easy to move through the day on auto-pilot. A schedule helps to make sure we commit to taking care of ourselves.

So for this next and final piece, I would like you to make a commitment to yourself to do a minimum of two things a day for your self-care. They don't have to be big things, but be sure to do them everyday to fill you up, to give to yourself, to show yourself the same love you do to others. You can use the space below, put reminders in your phone, or use a paper calendar–whatever the method, create a self-care schedule. Note what you will do for yourself each day and what time you will do it.
Write it down and commit to it:

MONTHLY *Self-Care* PLAN

MY PHYSICAL ACTIVITIES

NOTES

MON	TUE	WED	THU	FRI	SAT	SUN

This journey is a lifelong one. We will have setbacks and life ebbs and flows. We will continue to learn and honor ourselves in deeper ways on unexpected levels. In the space below, or on a separate piece of paper write a letter to your future self to read in a year.

Dear

Sincerely...

About the Author

Born in California and raised in Georgia, Kamryn Rock dealt with many hardships in her adolescence, eventually spending ten years in active addiction and leaving her homeless and shattered. In 2015, she experienced a life-changing event that projected her into a journey of recovery and wellness and helped develop within her a passion and drive to help others in similar struggles.

Grateful for her recovery, Kamryn returned to the center where she received treatment, this time to work with them to promote recovery, shape their program to best serve the individuals there, and give hope to those who were where she once stood.

To that end, Kamryn worked to become a Certified Addiction Counselor (CAC) and a Certified Addiction Recovery Empowerment Specialist (CARES), which led to her being selected as an ambassador working with the Georgia Council for Recovery to continue to promote recovery, provide hope, and shatter stigma on a statewide level.

Kamryn continues to dream big and push herself to grow in every way possible. The oldest of three siblings, she is the proud mother of three children of her own, a dedicated partner, a present force within her family, and an active member of her community.

Thank you!

Im extremely grateful for the support from each of you and time time you took in this workbook. What I am most grateful for is the work you are doing for yourself!

My hope for you is that-from my experience and walking this journey together-you have at least started to understand that you are enough and you are loved. I hope you have learned to see yourself in a different light. That you'll find it easier to set down those burdensome beliefs, judgments, fears, and insecurities that were never yours to carry. To be able to say, "I hear you, but not today".

I hope you'll be able to give yourself the same grace, compassion, understanding, and love that you show others around you. To be able to spend some time taking care of yourself and understand a little more about who you are at your core. To know that life is a journey and sometimes it's messy-and that's okay. To understand that you are not defined but what has happened to you, by the choices you have made. To understand you are a victor and not a victim.

I hope you are able to see the life and love you deserve. Able to fully live with wonder and awe, not tied to any negative thought, belief or past. I hope today you choose to love and honor yourself.

For more information, downloadable content, and life coaching please visit:
www.anchoredheartswellness.com

MY NOTES